YOU ARE MY WORLD

TÚ ERES MI MUNDO

YOU ARE MY WORLD

How a Parent's Love Shapes a Baby's Mind

TÚ ERES MI MUNDO

Cómo el amor de los padres forma la mente de un bebé

AMY HATKOFF

Traducción al español de Paola A. Soto

STEWART, TABORI & CHANG | NEW YORK

For parents everywhere, whose love has the power to change the world.
And for Grandmoe Doe, who changed mine.
With all my love to Juliana, Isabella, Lilly, Nina, Jack, Chloe,
Riley, Danielle and Alyson, who bring light to us everyday.

Para todos los padres, su amor tiene el poder de cambiar el mundo.
Y para Doe, mi abuela, quien cambió mi mundo. Con todo mi
amor a Juliana, Isabella, Lilly, Nina, Jack, Chloe, Riley, Danielle y
Alyson, que traen felicidad a nuestras vidas todos los días.

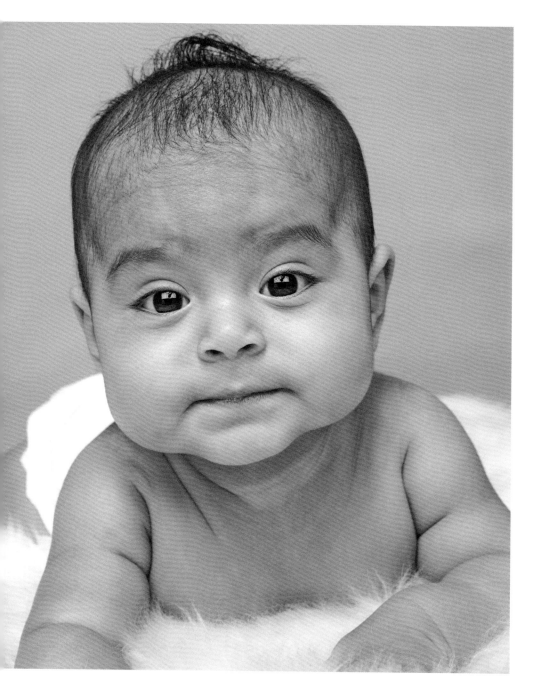

YOU ARE MY WORLD

celebrates the impact a parent's love and attention has on a baby's development. It portrays the significant role that small, everyday moments have in shaping a baby's sense of self and capacity to learn. Science tells us that the brain develops through the dance that occurs between parents and children. In this book, babies do the talking and ask parents to join them in the dance.

We know that children's minds are shaped by experience. The way we touch, hold, talk to, look at, and respond to a baby affects that baby's self-image, view of the world, and his or her role in it. We are sending messages to our babies all the time. It is the seemingly insignificant exchanges with the significant people in their lives that teach a child who he or she is and can become.

In the infinite wisdom of nature, the simple exchanges that occur in the give and take of the parent-child relationship do the very complex work of wiring the neural pathways in the baby's brain. There is now scientific evidence that the loving act of gazing into your baby's eyes, for example, helps to develop self-awareness and sensitivity to others. The warmth of your skin, the gentleness of your touch, the tone of your voice, the softness of your smile are all building blocks for your baby's healthy development. The minutes, hours and days spent loving your baby, making a fool of yourself talking in high-pitched voices, dancing together to your favorite tunes, or just sitting with your infant and cooing are worth their weight in gold. You are building the solid foundation for your baby's future.

The small dance steps of everyday experience create secure attachments, known to be essential for all aspects of healthy development. Yet, in our fast-paced world with its emphasis on success, independence, and achievement, babies are often pushed to be on their own before they are ready. Parents can be made to feel that the kind of responsiveness and attunement that builds secure attachments will spoil the baby and make the child too needy or dependent. The research tells us that the opposite is true—that we foster independence by meeting a baby's needs consistently and promptly. *You Are My World* explores the value of responding to your baby from your own heart and in your own rhythm.

The text, while often poetic, is based on the latest scientific research on infant brain development. For example, "Your love melts my fear," addresses the fact that loving interactions between parents and babies release oxytocin, the "love hormone." Oxytocin increases trust and new research demonstrates that sufficient production of this hormone in infancy is essential to the capacity to love throughout life. Simple gestures, lifelong benefits.

The words herein are written with profound respect for the power of a parent's love. They are meant to illuminate a baby's sheer delight in, desire for, and receptivity to that love. The unfolding and development of a baby is nothing short of a miracle. *You Are My World* celebrates the role of a parent's love in that miracle and captures the extraordinary impact of the "ordinary" acts of parenting.

TÚ ERES MI MUNDO celebra el impacto que el amor y la atención de los padres tiene sobre el desarrollo de su bebé. También demuestra la importancia que momentos pequeños, de cada día, tienen en la conformación de un sentido de sí mismo y la capacidad de aprender que tiene un bebé. La ciencia nos dice que el cerebro se desarrolla a través de la danza que se produce entre padres e hijos. En este libro, son los bebés que hablan y piden a los padres que se unan a ellos en la danza.

Sabemos que la mente de los niños se forma con la experiencia. La manera en que un padre toca, sostiene, habla, mira y responde a su bebé afecta la imagen que él o ella tiene de sí mismo, su visión del mundo y su papel en él. Los padres envían mensajes a sus bebés todo el tiempo. Es el intercambio aparentemente insignificante con las personas importantes en sus vidas que le enseña a un niño o niña lo que puede llegar a ser.

En la infinita sabiduría de la naturaleza, los simples intercambios que se producen en la relación entre padre e hijo ayudan a crear las complejas vías nerviosas en el cerebro del bebé. En la actualidad existe evidencia científica de que el acto amoroso de la mirada perdida en los ojos de su bebé, por ejemplo, ayuda a desarrollar la autoconciencia y sensibilidad hacia los demás. El calor de su piel, la delicadeza de su tacto, el tono de su voz, la suavidad de su sonrisa son todos bloques de construcción para el desarrollo saludable de su bebé. Los minutos, las horas y los días que pasan dándole cariño a su bebé, haciendo payasadas, hablando en voces chistosas, bailando juntos a sus canciones favoritas o simplemente estando presente con su bebé valen su peso en oro. Está construyendo un fundamento sólido para el futuro de su bebé.

Los pequeños pasos del baile de la experiencia cotidiana hacen vínculos seguros y sabemos que son esenciales para todos los aspectos del desarrollo sano. Sin embargo, en nuestro mundo de ritmo rápido, con énfasis en el éxito, la independencia y los logros, los bebés son empujados a estar solos antes de estar listos. Los padres pueden tener la sensación de que el tipo de respuesta y el entendimiento que construye una unión segura malcriará al bebé y lo hará demandante y dependiente. La investigación nos dice que ocurre todo lo contrario; el cumplimiento de las necesidades del bebé en una forma consistente y con inmediatez fomentan la independencia. *Tú eres mi mundo* explora el valor de responder a su bebé desde su propio corazón y en su propio ritmo.

El texto, aunque a menudo poético, se basa en las últimas investigaciones científicas sobre el desarrollo del cerebro infantil. Por ejemplo, "Tu amor derrite mi temor", responde al hecho de que las interacciones de amor entre los padres y los bebés son responsables de la liberación de oxitocina, "la hormona del amor". La oxitocina aumenta la confianza y una nueva investigación demuestra que la producción suficiente de esta hormona en la infancia es esencial para la capacidad de amar a través de toda la vida. Los gestos simples tienen beneficios que duran toda la vida.

Estas palabras se escriben aquí con un profundo respeto por el poder del amor de un padre. El propósito de este libro es iluminar el placer auténtico, el deseo y la receptividad de un bebé a ese amor. El despliegue y el desarrollo de un bebé es nada menos que un milagro. *Tú eres mi mundo* celebra el papel que el amor de un padre juega en ese milagro y captura el impacto extraordinario de los actos "normales" en la crianza de los hijos.

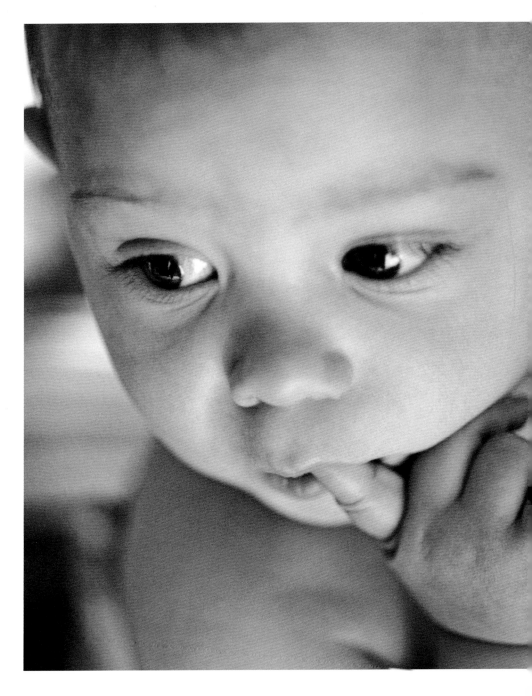

I KNOW YOU RIGHT FROM THE START.

I COULD PICK YOU OUT IN A CROWD.

TE CONOZCO DESDE EL PRINCIPIO.

TE PODRÍA ESCOGER EN UNA MULTITUD.

I AM BORN READY
TO CONNECT.

IT'S HOW I'M WIRED.

• •

YO NACÍ PREPARADO
PARA CONECTARME.

VINE ASÍ DE FÁBRICA.

YOUR LOVE IS
MY FIRST TEACHER.

♥

TU AMOR ES MI
PRIMER MAESTRO.

WHEN I CAN COUNT ON YOU,
I LEARN TO TRUST.

■ ■ ■ ■ ■ ■

CUANDO PUEDO CONTAR CONTIGO,
APRENDO A CONFIAR.

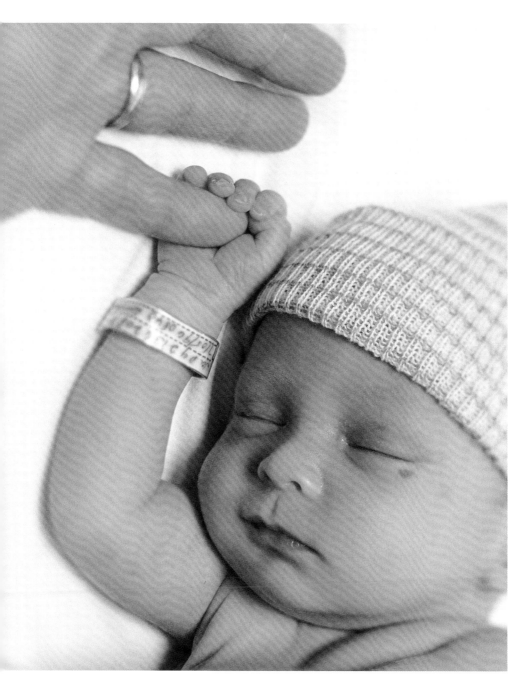

THE FIRST MILESTONE

Learning to trust is the main developmental task of the first year of life. When a baby learns to trust during this period, his or her brain will be wired to trust throughout life. Trust develops when a baby can count on his or her needs being met, knows that a parent is emotionally available, and has soothing routines. Responsive, sensitive parenting gives a baby's brain the message that the world is a safe place and that people are dependable.

EL PRIMER HITO

Aprender a confiar es la tarea principal en el desarrollo del primer año de vida. En este periodo, cuando un bebé aprende a confiar de recién nacido, el cerebro de ese bebé aprende a tener confianza durante el resto de su vida. La confianza se desarrolla cuando un bebé puede contar con la satisfacción de sus necesidades, sabe que un padre está disponible emocional-mente y tiene rutinas relajadoras. Los padres que son responsables y sensibles les dan al cerebro de su bebé el mensaje de que el mundo es un lugar seguro y que las personas son confiables.

WHEN YOU UNDERSTAND ME,
YOU HELP ME TO
UNDERSTAND THE WORLD.

CUANDO TÚ ME COMPRENDES,
ME AYUDAS
A COMPRENDER EL MUNDO.

YOU ARE MY MIRROR.

YOU ARE MY MIRROR.

TÚ ERES MI ESPEJO.

TÚ ERES MI ESPEJO.

WHEN YOU SMILE AT ME,
I LEARN THAT I AM LOVABLE.

CUANDO TÚ ME SONRÍES,
YO APRENDO QUE SOY ADORABLE.

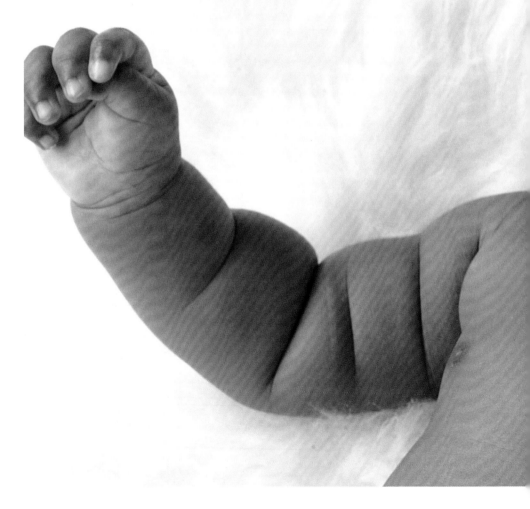

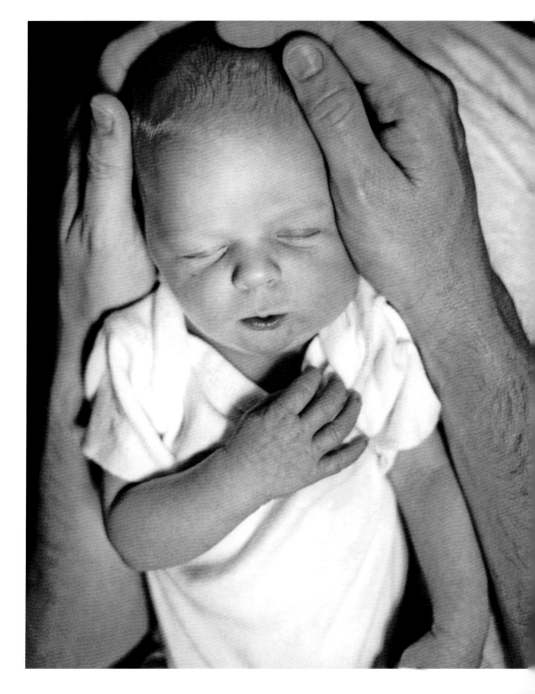

YOUR TOUCH IS LIKE MAGIC.
IT HELPS ME DEVELOP IN EVERY WAY.

TU TACTO ES COMO MAGIA.
ME AYUDA A DESARROLLAR TODO
LOS ASPECTOS DE MI SER.

WHEN YOU HOLD ME, I FEEL SAFE AND SECURE.

CUANDO TÚ ME SUJETAS,
YO ME SIENTO SANO Y SALVO.

**THE STRONGER OUR BOND,
THE STRONGER I BECOME.**

**CUANTO MÁS FUERTE SE
HACE NUESTRA CONEXIÓN,
MÁS FUERTE LLEGO A SER.**

YOU ARE MY ANCHOR.

—

TÚ ERES MI ANCLA.

A SECURE ATTACHMENT: THE KEY TO SUCCESS

Research now tells us that the single most important factor in shaping a child's future is the quality of the attachment to the parent. It has been confirmed that children who have secure attachments to their parents have more positive outcomes in a range of areas including personality development, learning, and the ability to form healthy relationships.

A seminal study demonstrated that babies who are held often and are securely attached to their parents in the first six months of life do not show elevated levels of cortisol, the stress hormone, in subsequent stressful situations. Stress is now known to be harmful to the development of brain cells. A nurturing relationship protects children from the impact of stress and helps them manage challenges throughout life.

LA CLAVE DEL ÉXITO:
UN CARIÑO SEGURO

Hay estudios que dicen que el factor más importante en la formación del futuro de un bebé es la calidad de unión que tiene con sus padres. Se ha confirmado que los niños que tienen una conexión segura con sus padres tienen resultados positivos en más de una área, incluyendo el desarrollo de su personalidad, el aprendizaje y la capacidad para formar relaciones sanas.

Un estudio seminal demostró que los bebés que están firmemente conectados con sus padres y son agarrados con frecuencia en los primeros seis meses de sus vidas no presentan niveles elevados de cortisol, la hormona del estrés, en posteriores situaciones de estrés. Hoy es conocido que el estrés puede ser perjudicial para el desarrollo de las células cerebrales. Una relación afectiva protege a los niños de los efectos del estrés y ayuda a manejar los desafíos a través de la vida.

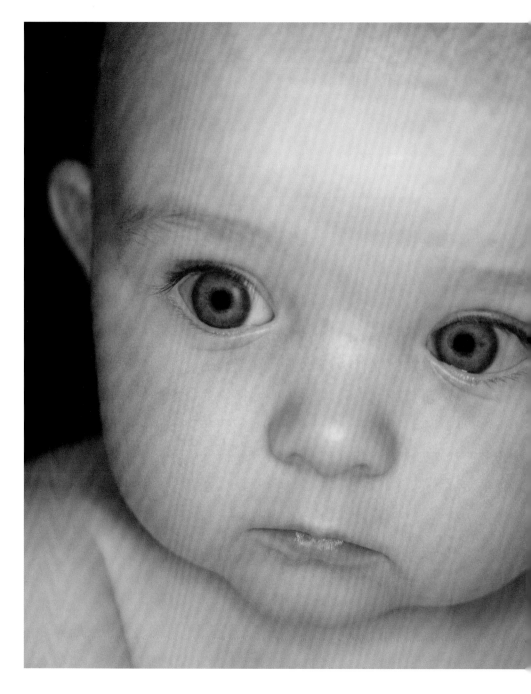

IT TAKES TIME FOR ME TO LEARN THAT
I WILL BE OKAY WITHOUT YOU.

TOMA TIEMPO PARA QUE YO APRENDA
QUE VOY A ESTAR BIEN SIN TI.

I MAY BE SMALL, BUT I FEEL IT ALL.

SOY PEQUEÑO, PERO LO SIENTO TODO.

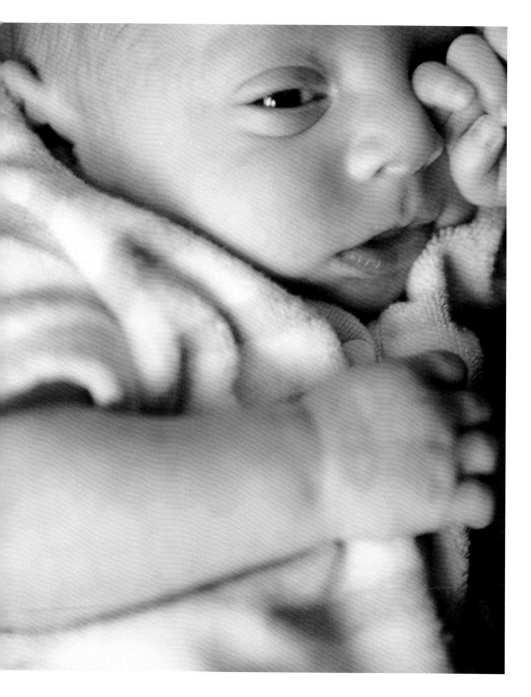

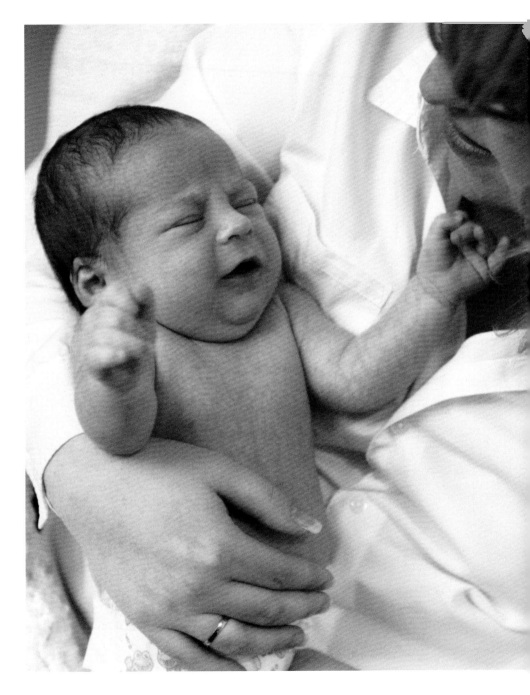

LOUD SOUNDS, BRIGHT LIGHT,
OR JUST BEING UNDRESSED CAN
OVERWHELM ME.

SONIDOS FUERTES, LUCES BRILLANTES,
O SIMPLEMENTE ESTAR DESNUDO
ME PUEDE AGOBIAR.

WHEN I AM HUNGRY,
I COME UNDONE.

**CUANDO TENGO HAMBRE
ME DESHAGO.**

WHEN YOU KISS MY BOO-BOOS,
YOU TEACH ME HOW TO BE KIND
TOWARD OTHERS.

CUANDO ME BESAS LAS HERIDAS,
ME ENSEÑAS A SER AMABLE
CON OTROS.

YOU ARE MY BUFFER.
YOU PROTECT ME FROM ALL THE NEWNESS.

TÚ ERES MI AMORTIGUADOR.
ME PROTEGES DE TODO LO NUEVO.

WHEN I AM CRYING,
I HOPE YOU WILL COME.

I DON'T KNOW HOW
TO MAKE IT BETTER BY
MYSELF.

CUANDO LLORO ESPERO
QUE TE ACERQUES.

NO SÉ CÓMO HACERME
SENTIR MEJOR SOLO.

YOU CAN'T SPOIL ME

There has long been controversy about whether or not picking up a crying baby will spoil him or her. In a survey conducted by Zero to Three: The National Center, it was found that 47 percent of adults think that you will spoil infants under three months if you pick them up every time they cry. While this belief is prevalent in many cultures, it is in conflict with research findings that tell us the more we respond to babies' needs, the less needy they will become.

A groundbreaking study demonstrated that children whose cries are met consistently and promptly in the first quarter of the first year, cry less and sleep better in the rest of the that year. The study also found that babies whose cries elicit responses tend to develop into independent, confident, and self-reliant children.

TÚ NO ME PUEDES MALCRIAR

Desde hace tiempo ha habido una controversia acerca de si cargar a un bebé que está llorando puede o no malcriarlo. En una encuesta realizada por Zero to Three: The National Center, se comprobó que el 47% de los adultos piensa que recoger a un bebé menor de tres meses, cada vez que llora, lo malcría. Mientras esta creencia es frecuente en muchas culturas, está en conflicto con las conclusiones de investigaciones que nos demuestran que cuanto más respondemos a las necesidades de los bebés, menos demandantes serán.

Un estudio innovador demostró que los niños que han sido atendidos de inmediato y sistemáticamente al llorar durante el primer trimestre del año, lloran menos y duermen mejor durante el resto de ese mismo año. El estudio también encontró que los bebés que lloran y provocan respuestas de sus padres, terminan siendo hijos independientes y seguros.

I KNOW WHAT I LIKE...

¡YO SÉ LO QUE ME GUSTA...

...AND WHAT I DON'T!
...Y LO QUE NO ME GUSTA!

READ YOUR BABY

Research shows that reading and responding to a baby's cues are more important to brain development than any structured learning activity. Babies who feel understood learn more easily, have a positive sense of self, develop empathy, and can decipher social cues of others. As babies are seen, understood, and felt, they begin to experience and have a greater awareness of who they are.

LEA A SU BEBÉ

Las investigaciones muestran que leer y responder a las señales de su bebé es más importante para el desarrollo del cerebro que cualquier actividad educativa. Los bebés que sienten que sus padres los comprenden aprenden más fácilmente, tienen un sentido positivo de sí mismo, desarrollan empatía y pueden descifrar las señales sociales de los demás. Cuando los bebés sienten que alguien los observa y entiende, ellos comienzan a tener una mayor conciencia de lo que son.

I LOVE BABY MASSAGE.
IT KEEPS ME CALM, HELPS
ME TO SLEEP, AND BRINGS
ME CLOSER TO YOU

ADORO LOS MASAJES PARA
BEBÉS. ME MANTIENEN
TRANQUILO, ME AYUDAN
A DORMIR Y ME HACEN
SENTIR MÁS CERCA DE TI.

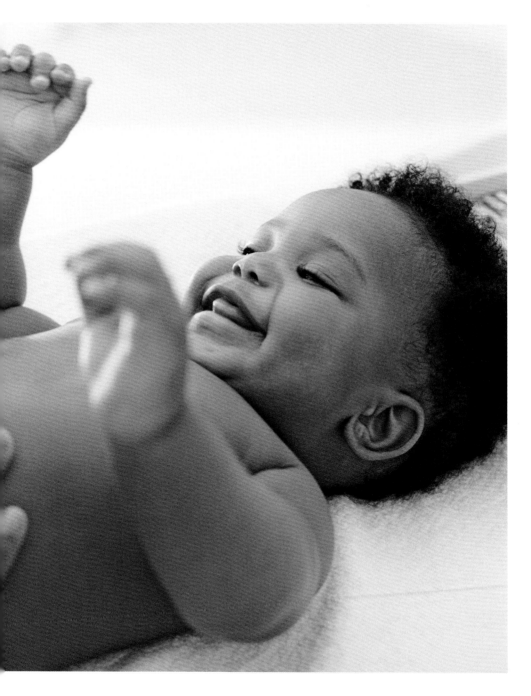

TOO MUCH STRESS
CAN BE TOXIC TO MY BRAIN.

DEMASIADO ESTRÉS PUEDE SER
TÓXICO A MI CEREBRO.

YOUR LOVE
MELTS MY FEAR.

♥

TU AMOR DERRITE
MI TEMOR.

WHEN YOU LEAVE,
I WORRY THAT YOU WON'T
COME BACK.

I AM JUST LEARNING THAT
I WILL SEE YOU AGAIN.

■ ■ ■ ■

CUANDO TE VAS
ME PREOCUPA QUE NO
VAYAS A REGRESAR.

TODAVÍA ESTOY
APRENDIENDO QUE
TE VOLVERÉ A VER.

I'M A MIMIC.

SHOW ME AND
I WILL FOLLOW!

¡SOY UN MÍMICO,
MUÉSTRAME Y
YO TE SEGUIRÉ!

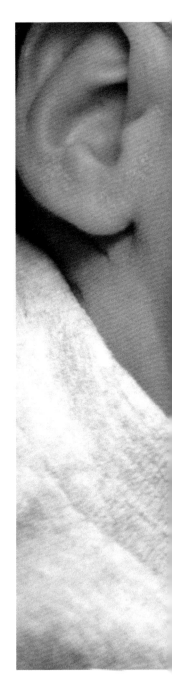

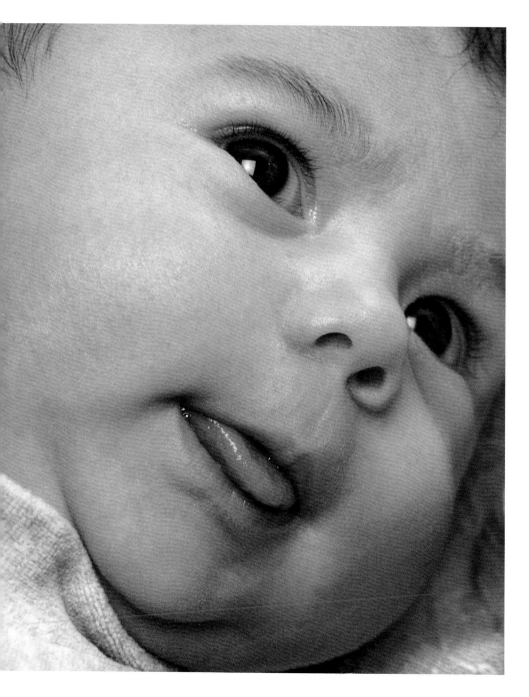

LOVING EXCHANGES
LAST A LIFETIME

Loving interactions between parents
and babies release oxytocin, commonly
referred to as the "love hormone."
Oxytocin reduces stress and increases
trust. Recent research has demonstrated
that the sufficient production of oxytocin
in infancy is essential to the capacity to
maintain healthy interpersonal relationships throughout life.

INTERCAMBIOS CARIÑOSOS
DURAN UNA VIDA ENTERA

Intercambios cariñosos entre padres y bebés
liberan oxitocina, comúnmente denominada
"la hormona del amor". La oxitocina reduce
el estrés y aumenta la confianza. Recientes
investigaciones han demostrado que la producción suficiente de oxitocina en la infancia
es esencial para la capacidad de mantener
relaciones interpersonales sanas a través
de la vida.

I LEARN FROM EVERYTHING I DO.

APRENDO DE TODO LO QUE HAGO.

WHEN I SAY "OOOHH," AND YOU
SAY "AAAHH," WE'RE TALKING.

CUANDO YO DIGO "OOOHH" Y TÚ
DICES "AAAHH", ESTAMOS HABLANDO.

WHEN WE "GET DOWN"
TOGETHER AND PLAY, I LEARN HOW
TO PLAY IN THE WORLD.

CUANDO JUGAMOS JUNTOS, APRENDO
CÓMO JUGAR EN EL MUNDO.

**WHEN YOU GET EXCITED ABOUT ME,
I GET EXCITED ABOUT LIFE.**

**CUANDO TE EMOCIONAS AL VERME,
YO ME EMOCIONO CON LA VIDA.**

YOUR LOVE
GIVES ME WINGS.

TU AMOR
ME DA ALAS.

WHEN YOU FOLLOW MY LEAD,
YOU HELP ME TO BECOME A LEADER.

—

CUANDO TÚ ME SIGUES,
ME ENSEÑAS A SER UN LÍDER.

LAYING A STRONG FOUNDATION

Comforting responses from adults help babies develop the capacity to soothe and calm themselves. This capacity is considered to be a cornerstone for emotional, social and cognitive development, impacting such areas as concentration, attention, and the understanding of oneself and others.

THE POWER OF PLAY

The give and take of playing helps babies develop and learn about themselves, the world and relationships. Babies learn best when adults allow them to be the leader and respond in ways that expand upon their play.

COMIENZA CON UNA BASE FUERTE

Cuando los adultos responden cariñosamente, ayudan a que los bebés desarrollen la capacidad para aliviar y calmarse a sí mismos. Esta capacidad en los bebés se considera un fundamento importantísimo para su desarrollo social, emocional y mental, ya que afecta áreas como la concentración, la atención y la comprensión de uno mismo y de los demás.

EL PODER DE JUGAR

El dar y recibir en el juego ayuda a los bebés a que desarrollen y aprendan acerca de sí mismos, el mundo y las relaciones. Los bebés aprenden mejor cuando los adultos les permiten ser el líder y responden de una manera donde amplían su juego.

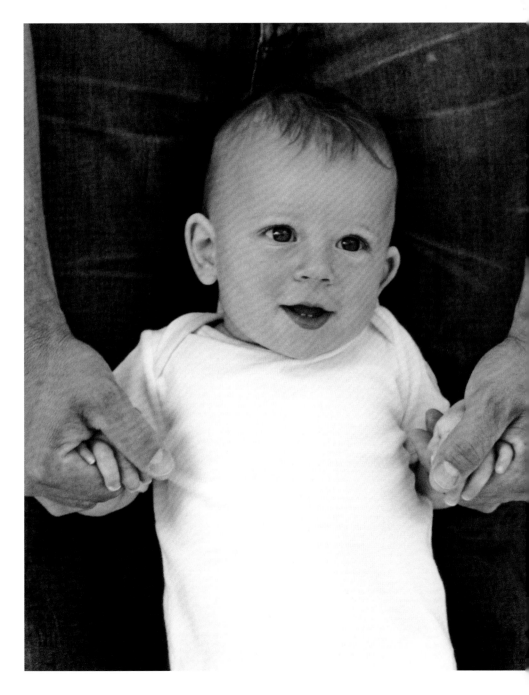

WITH YOU BEHIND ME, I FEEL SAFE
ENOUGH TO TRY NEW THINGS.

CON TU RESPALDO, ME SIENTO SEGURO
PARA PROBAR COSAS NUEVAS.

WHEN I CAN LEAN ON YOU,
I LEARN TO STAND ON MY OWN.

•

CUANDO PUEDO APOYARME EN TI,
APRENDO A PARARME SOLO.

WHAT YOU GIVE TO ME,
I CAN GIVE TO OTHERS.

LO QUE TÚ ME DAS A MÍ,
YO LE PUEDO DAR A OTROS.

**NOBODY KNOWS ME
BETTER THAN YOU.**

**NADIE ME CONOCE
MEJOR QUE TI.**

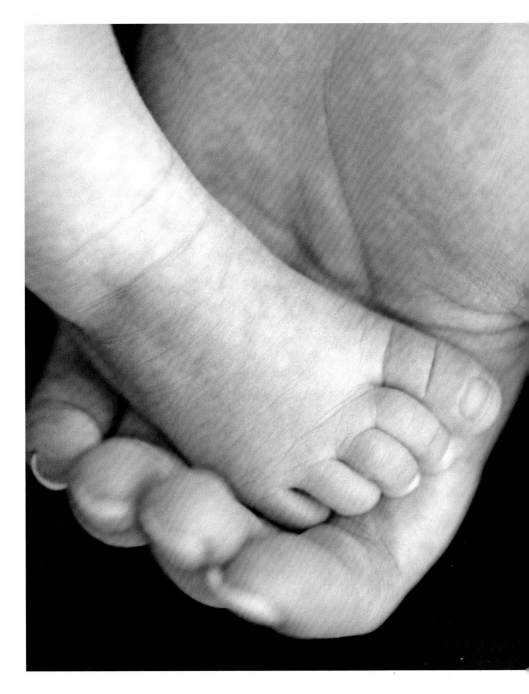

YOUR LOVE PREPARES ME
FOR THE JOURNEY.

TU AMOR ME PREPARA
PARA EL VIAJE.

RECOMMENDED RESOURCES

BOOKS

Bowlby, John. *A Secure Base: Parent-Child Attachment and Healthy Human Development.* London: Basic Books, 1988.

Barnet, M.D., Ann B. and Richard J. Barnet. *The Youngest Minds; Parenting and Genes in the Development of Intellect and Emotion.* New York: Simon & Schuster, 1998.

Elliot, Lise. *What's Going on in There? How the Brain and Mind Develop in the First Five Years of Life.* New York: Bantam, 1999.

Gerhardt, Sue. *Why Love Matters: How Affection Shapes a Baby's Brain.* New York: Brunner-Routledge, 2004.

Heller, Sharon. *The Vital Touch: How Intimate Contact With Your Baby Leads to Happier, Healthier Development.* New York: Henry Holt & Company, 1997.

Johnson & Johnson Pediatric Institute, *The Importance of Touch.* Cincinnati: Johnson & Johnson Pediatric Institute.

Johnson & Johnson Pediatric Institute and Zero to Three, *The Magic of Everyday Moments.* Zero to Three, 2000.

Karen Ph.D., Robert. *Becoming Attached: First Relationships and How They Shape Our Capacity to Love.* New York: Warner Books, 1994.

Lief, Nina R. and Mary Ellen Fahs (ed). *The First Year of Life: A Guide to Parenting.* New York: Walker and Company, 1991.

McClure, Vimala. *Infant Massage: A Handbook for Loving Parents.* New York: Bantam, 2000.

Montagu, Ashley. *Touching: The Human Significance of Skin.* New York: Harper and Row, 1986.

Pruett, Kyle. *Fatherneed: Why Father Care Is as Essential as Mother Care for Your Child.* New York: The Free Press, 2000.

Stern, Daniel N. *The Birth of a Mother: How the Motherhood Experience Changes You Forever.* New York: Basic Books, 1999.

Stern, Daniel N. *Diary of a Baby.* New York: Basic Books, 1990, 1998.

VIDEOS AND DVDS

Amazing Talents of the Newborn, Johnson & Johnson Pediatric Institute

Begin with Love, hosted by Oprah Winfrey, Civitas

Ten Things Every Child Needs for the Best Start in Life! T. Berry Brazelton

The Baby Human, Geniuses in Diapers

The First Years Last Forever, hosted by Rob Reiner, I Am Your Child Video Series

To Be A Father, hosted by Ray Romano, I Am Your Child Video Series

RECOMMENDED WEB SITES

Civitas
(www.civitas.org)

Parents' Action of Children
(www.parentsaction.org)

International Institute of Infant Massage
(www.infantmassageinstitute.com)

Johnson & Johnson Pediatric Institute
(www.jjpi.net)

Zero to Three: The National Center
(www.zerotothree.org)

RECURSOS RECOMENDADOS

LIBROS

Bowlby, John. *A Secure Base: Parent-Child Attachment and Healthy Human Development.* London: Basic Books, 1988.

Barnet, M.D., Ann B. y Richard J. Barnet. *The Youngest Minds; Parenting and Genes in the Development of Intellect and Emotion.* New York: Simon & Schuster, 1998.

Elliot, Lise. *What's Going on in There? How the Brain and Mind Develop in the First Five Years of Life.* New York: Bantam, 1999.

Gerhardt, Sue. *Why Love Matters: How Affection Shapes a Baby's Brain.* New York: Brunner-Routledge, 2004.

Heller, Sharon. *The Vital Touch: How Intimate Contact With Your Baby Leads to Happier, Healthier Development.* New York: Henry Holt & Company, 1997.

Johnson & Johnson Pediatric Institute, *The Importance of Touch.* Cincinnati: Johnson & Johnson Pediatric Institute.

Johnson & Johnson Pediatric Institute y Zero to Three, *The Magic of Everyday Moments.* Zero to Three, 2000.

Karen Ph.D., Robert. *Becoming Attached: First Relationships and How They Shape Our Capacity to Love.* New York: Warner Books, 1994.

Lief, Nina R. y Mary Ellen Fahs (ed). *The First Year of Life: A Guide to Parenting.* New York: Walker and Company, 1991.

McClure, Vimala. *Infant Massage: A Handbook for Loving Parents.* New York: Bantam, 2000.

Montagu, Ashley. *Touching: The Human Significance of Skin.* New York: Harper and Row, 1986.

Pruett, Kyle. *Fatherneed: Why Father Care Is as Essential as Mother Care for Your Child.* New York: The Free Press, 2000.

Stern, Daniel N. *The Birth of a Mother: How the Motherhood Experience Changes You Forever.* New York: Basic Books, 1999.

Stern, Daniel N. *Diary of a Baby.* New York: Basic Books, 1990, 1998.

VIDEOS Y DVDS

Amazing Talents of the Newborn, Johnson & Johnson Pediatric Institute

Begin with Love, presentado por Oprah Winfrey, Civitas

Ten Things Every Child Needs for the Best Start in Life! T. Berry Brazelton

The Baby Human, Geniuses in Diapers

The First Years Last Forever, presentado por Rob Reiner, I Am Your Child Video Series

To Be A Father, presentado por Ray Romano, I Am Your Child Video Series

PÁGINAS WEB

Civitas
(www.civitas.org)

Parents' Action of Children
(www.parentsaction.org)

International Institute of Infant Massage
(www.infantmassageinstitute.com)

Johnson & Johnson Pediatric Institute
(www.jjpi.net)

Zero to Three: The National Center
(www.zerotothree.org)

ACKNOWLEDGMENTS

THERE ARE SO MANY PEOPLE WHO HAVE INSPIRED THIS BOOK and helped to bring it into the world. I'd like to acknowledge the countless mothers I have worked with who, despite the lack of support in their lives or struggles in their own childhoods, came to my programs with open hearts and minds, wanting to give their children the love and understanding they may never have received. I'd like to thank Doris and Leon Hatkoff, who taught me about a parent's ability to focus on their children with a tenacious generosity and an infinite capacity for being available, supportive and loving. And to the entire Hatkoff clan, especially my siblings, Susan and Craig, and their spouses and their spouses' families, who all share the ability to pour love, opportunities and sweetness into their children, a tradition I revel in seeing pass down through the generations. A very special thank you to Juliana and Isabella, who have taught me about the power of love from the moment they were born. And my warmest welcome and thanks to Jack, Chloe and Riley, whose beautiful spirits are steady reminders of how a parent's love helps a child grow.

My deepest thanks to Chris Culler, Tom Harriman, Dorothy Henderson, Sonia Orenstein, Gay French-Ottaviani, and Victoria Patricof for their input, edits and expertise; the Institute for Infants, Children & Families of the Jewish Board of Family and Children's Services for their nurturing and extraordinary training; Wendy Sarasohn and Ellen Whyte, my personal *doulas*, who encouraged this production from the start; Marcia Patricof for her feedback and hospitality, both of which helped me reach the finish line; and Annie Abram whose brilliance and friendship continually fuel my creativity. And finally, many thanks to Carolyn French for her enthusiasm and commitment to delivering *You Are My World* and to Marisa Bulzone for being the midwife.

ABOUT THE AUTHOR

AMY HATKOFF is a parenting educator, writer, filmmaker, and advocate. She has been working with parents and children of diverse backgrounds for more than 20 years. In 1995, she was asked to translate the groundbreaking research on infant brain development into an accessible language for parents for Rob Reiner's widely acclaimed video *The First Years Last Forever*. She has brought that information to hundreds of parents, teachers, and caregivers through seminars and lectures in hospitals, corporations, doctor's offices, schools, welfare hotels, homeless shelters, and community organizations. She is co-producer of the award-winning documentary *Neglect Not The Children*, and co-author of *How to Save the Children*. Ms. Hatkoff is a graduate of the Institute for Infants, Children & Families, the Parenting Education and Family Support program of Wheelock College, and Hamilton College.

AGRADECIMIENTOS

HAY MUCHAS PERSONAS QUE HAN INSPIRADO ESTE LIBRO y ayudaron a traerlo al mundo. Me gustaría agradecer a las madres innumerables con quien yo trabajé: a pesar de la falta de apoyo en sus vidas o las luchas en su propia infancia, llegaron a mis programas con sus corazones y mentes abiertos, con ganas de dar a sus hijos el amor y la comprensión que nunca recibieron. Me gustaría dar las gracias a Doris y Leon Hatkoff, quienes me enseñaron la capacidad que tiene un padre para dirigir su atención a sus niños con una gran generosidad y una disposición infinita para brindar apoyo y amor y estar disponible. A todos los miembros de la familia Hatkoff, especialmente a mi hermana y hermano, Susan y Craig, sus cónyuges, y sus propias familias, que comparten la habilidad de dar amor, oportunidades y cariño a sus hijos. Me da mucho gusto ver esta tradición pasar de una generación a otra. Un agradecimiento muy especial a Juliana e Isabella, que me han enseñado sobre el poder del amor desde el momento en que nacieron. Y mi más cordial bienvenida y gracias a Jack, Chloe y Riley, sus espíritus hermosos me recuerdan constantemente cómo el amor de los padres ayuda a un niño a crecer.

Mi más profundo agradecimiento a Chris Culler, Tom Harriman, Dorothy Henderson, Sonia Orenstein, Gay French-Ottaviani y Victoria Patricof por sus consejos, revisiones y sus experiencias; al Institute for Infants, Children & Families of the Jewish Board of Family and Children's Services por su apoyo y entrenamiento extraordinario; a Wendy Sarasohn y Ellen Whyte, mi doulas personales, quien tuvieron fe en esta producción desde el principio; a Marcia Patricof por sus observaciones y por la hospitalidad, ambas de las cuales me ayudaron a llegar a la línea final; a Annie Abram, que con su genialidad y amistad continúa alimentando mi creatividad. Y, por último, muchas gracias a Carolyn French por su entusiasmo y compromiso a atender el parto de *Tú eres mi mundo* y a Marisa Bulzone por ser la partera.

ACERCA DE LA AUTORA

AMY HATKOFF es una educadora de padres, escritora, cineasta y defensora de niños. Ella ha estado trabajando con padres y niños de diversos orígenes hace más de veinte años. En 1995 se le pidió que tradujera la investigación pionera en el desarrollo cerebral infantil a un lenguaje accesible para los padres, para un vídeo que fue extensamente aclamado, *The First Years Last Forever*, dirigido por Rob Reiner. Ella ha traído esta información a cientos de padres, maestros y cuidadores a través de seminarios y conferencias en los hospitales, las corporaciones, los consultorios médicos, las escuelas, los hoteles de bienestar, los refugios para desamparados y las organizaciones comunitarias. Es una de los productores del documental *Neglect Not the Children*, el cual ganó un premio, y una de los escritores del libro *How to Save the Children*. La señorita Hatkoff se graduó del programa Institute for Infants, Children & Families, the Parenting Education and Family Support de Wheelock College y de Hamilton College.

Published in 2010
by Stewart, Tabori & Chang
An imprint of ABRAMS

Publicado en 2010
por Stewart, Tabori & Chang
Una impresión de ABRAMS

ISBN 978-1-58479-919-1

Editor: Marisa Bulzone
Design: LeAnna Weller Smith
Bilingual-edition design: Shawn Dahl, dahlimama inc
Production manager: Anet Sirna-Bruder

The text of this book was composed in Avenir

Printed and bound in China

10 9 8 7 6 5 4 3 2 1

ABRAMS
THE ART OF BOOKS SINCE 1949

115 West 18th Street
New York, NY 10011
www.abramsbooks.com